# Seeking Higher Ground

# Seeking Higher Ground

**Set your mind on things above, not on earthly things**

A 21 Day Spiritual Journey

*When you know it's time to move to another level-
it's time to seek higher ground.*

*Evangelist Norma J. Faith Walker Bean*

Copyright © 2009 by Norma J. Bean.

ISBN:         Hardcover         978-1-4415-4039-3
                 Softcover          978-1-4415-4038-6

All rights reserved. No part of this book may be reproduced or transmitted in any form or by any means, electronic or mechanical, including photocopying, recording, or by any information storage and retrieval system, without permission in writing from the copyright owner.

This book was printed in the United States of America.

**To order additional copies of this book, contact:**
Xlibris Corporation
1-888-795-4274
www.Xlibris.com
Orders@Xlibris.com
61472

# *FOREWORD*

It is my pleasure to present a forward to this meaningful text. I believe that this work has the potential to be a tremendous resource for the Body of Christ.

The most important relationship in our lives is our relationship with the Lord. Like every other relationship, our relationship with the Lord requires attention. We must continuously pray to communicate and maintain our connection with God. We must also study and meditate on God's word in order to grow in our relationship with the Lord.

With this work, Evangelist Norma J. Faith Walker Bean has provided a timely resource to help the people of God grow closer to God. The 21 daily meditations featured in this writing cover a broad range of topics that will inspire, instruct, and challenge the reader. Aptly focusing on the "Higher Ground" theme, Evangelist Bean ushers us into a greater awareness of and appreciation for the power and presence of God in our lives. It is through this awareness, and the deeper relationship with the Lord that results from this awareness, that we are able to make our way to the higher ground.

Life is challenging and the higher ground we seek may seem so far away. Nevertheless, in all things, God works for the good of those who love Him and who have been called according to His purpose.

The Lord is faithful and will undoubtedly do what He said he would do. It is up to us to do our part by taking advantage of opportunities the Lord presents to us, through resources such as this, to seek a closer walk with Him, which, in turn, will lead us to Higher Ground.

Pastor Gerald A. Cooper
St. James African Methodist Episcopal Church
Cleveland, Ohio

# *"SEEKING HIGHER GROUND"*

# *A TWENTY-ONE DAY SPIRITUAL JOURNEY*

**Colossians 3:1-2**
Since, then, you have been raised with Christ, set your hearts on things above, where Christ is seated at the right hand of God. Set your minds on things above, not on earthly things. (NIV)

Why did I choose twenty-one days for this journey? Well, social scientist and sociologist tell us that if we purposely and intentionally do something daily for twenty-one days, we begin to form a habit. Prayerfully, at the completion of your twenty-one days, you will cultivate a desire to spend at least fifteen minutes a day in meditation with the Lord. I also chose twenty-one days, because Daniel waited twenty-one days before he received the answer to his prayer. (Read Daniel 10$^{th}$ Chapter) It did not take twenty-one days for God to send an answer to Daniel's prayer, but a spiritual battle in the heavenly places delayed the answer from reaching Daniel. Nevertheless, Daniel was constant in prayer until he received his answer from God.

We may have to wait on the answer to our prayers. James 5:16b tells us, "The effectual fervent prayer of the righteous availith much." Whether our answer arrives quickly, or at a later time, we pray *in faith* that God will answer in His perfect timing. Remember: He's working, while we are waiting!

The Apostle Paul advises us to seek or look for things above, where Christ sits. He further says, "Set your minds on things above, not on earthly things." As we embark on this twenty-one day spiritual journey, **SEEKING HIGHER GROUND**, look up to God to empower us to reach higher ground.

This project has been a tremendous joy for me to write. I sought the Holy Spirit's leading and guidance in each meditation. God knew *you* would be using this for your edification, so it was written with **you** in the mind of Christ. Begin each meditation by setting your mind on things above, breathing deeply the breath of God, and writing your sincerest thoughts and reflections.

May God bless you abundantly as you grow in the knowledge of Christ and continue on your spiritual journey.

Special thank you and my deepest love to my husband, Rev. Dr. Elmo A. Bean, for his encouragement and support. Thank you also, to my daughters: Hope, Terri, Mercedes, and Norma Jean, for their encouragement and support.

# CONTENTS

Unsearchable Things Of God ................................................. 11
Be Generous And Be Refreshed ............................................ 13
God Carried Me ..................................................................... 15
Treasures In Clay .................................................................. 17
Room For You ....................................................................... 19
Shut The Door ....................................................................... 22
God Still Moves Stones ......................................................... 25
Be An Encourager ................................................................. 27
All Knowing God .................................................................... 29
His Blessing .......................................................................... 31
Step Out ................................................................................ 33
The Blessing ......................................................................... 35
Blessed Faithfulness ............................................................. 39
Praise And Thanksgiving ...................................................... 41
Examine Your Fruit ............................................................... 43
It's Within You ....................................................................... 45
There Is A Champion In You ................................................. 47
Intercessors .......................................................................... 49
This Time He Came Down .................................................... 51
The Call ................................................................................. 53
Humble Your Soul ................................................................. 55

# *UNSEARCHABLE THINGS OF GOD*

**Jeremiah 33: 2-3**
"This is what the Lord says, He who made the earth, the Lord who formed it and established it-the Lord is His name; "Call to me and I will answer you and tell you great and unsearchable things you do not know."

We presently live in, what is known as, "The Information Age". Sattlelights and computers have opened avenues to receive all kinds of information in a matter of seconds. Students can view a screen and be taught by someone in another country thousands of miles away. Through computers, information can be accessed on any subject simply by the click of a "mouse". yet some things can still only be revealed by God. What are these "great and unsearchable things?"

There are spiritual principles we need to help us mature in the faith. God knows what each one of us needs to help us navigate the vicissitudes of life. These are some of the things that only God can reveals to us. To know how to live an abundant life, how to love your enemies, how to walk in integrity, how to speak words of life, how to be empowered to share with those in need, career moves, and every thing in the spiritual realm-then call on the name of the Lord.

The prophet Jeremiah reminds us that, the Lord made the earth, formed it, and established it. We are further reminded that the earth is the Lords, the fullness thereof, the world and they that dwell within." That's reason enough to, call on the name of the Lord. He is waiting to answer your every prayer.

# MY THOUGHTS AND MEDITATION

# *BE GENEROUS AND BE REFRESHED*

**Proverbs 11:25**
"A generous man(woman) will prosper; he (she) who refreshes others will themselves be refreshed."

The first part of this proverb should give everyone pause. Being generous appears to have gone out of vogue. We hear televangelist and others espousing prosperity messages on how to *get* money and how to *gain material goods*. But once you become prosperous, there is no mention of sharing of your wealth with the less fortunate; yet we read further in Luke 6:38, "Give, and it will be given to you. a good measure, pressed down, shaken together and running over, will be poured into your lap. For with the measure you use, will be measured to you." Just image-pressed down (mashing down so more can get in),shaken together (so even more can get in), running over (wow). These are encouraging words for us to truly be generous! Today let's ask God to help us be generous.

Omnipotent, Omnipresent, Omnicient God, Give me a generous spirit. Lift my hands to pour into someone's life and spirit, who needs refreshing today. Empower me to refresh others, whereby I too may be refreshed.

In Jesus' name. Amen.

## MY THOUGHTS AND MEDITATION

# GOD CARRIED ME

**Exodus 19:4**
"You yourselves have seen what I did to Egypt, and how I carried you on eagles wings and brought you to myself."

There have been situations in each of our lives where, when we look back, we are amazed at the way God provided for us. Maybe God kept you from a dangerous situation or put you in a wonderful situation, whereby you knew it was God alone, whose hand was upon you.

January 17th, 2007, I was in a car accident on an icy highway, where my car spun out, turned me into on-coming traffic and slammed me into a concrete wall—yet I walked away-unharmed. As this was taking place, all I could yell was, "Jesus, Jesus, Jesus." But more miraculously, my car was not even damaged! A simi-truck traveling behind me, saw me spin out, was able to stop and held up traffic as I turned around. In relating this story to my spiritual sister, I said, "I can't understand how I could be slammed into a concrete wall, not be hurt nor my car damaged." She replied, "You did not hit the wall. God threw up a barrier and that is what you hit." Yes-God let me see that He carried me on eagles wings and brought me to himself. What is your testimony? It may not be as dramatic, yet you know, God carried you and brought you to Himself.

Take a few moments to reflect on the way God brought you to Himself, and be thankful.

## MY THOUGHTS AND MEDITATION

# *TREASURES IN CLAY*

**2 Corinthians 4:7**
But we have this treasure in jars of clay to show that this all surpassing power is from God and not from us.

What a blessing-to be called "A Treasure." The prophet Jeremiah tells the story of the potters house, in the 18th Chapter (vs.6) This story is an analogy of God shaping and reshaping man. Have you ever been cracked up, bent out of shape and twisted by the world? Have you come to the realization that at some point in your life you need to be put back on the Potters wheel? One glorious day, I knew I needed to be back on the Potters wheel. That was when I was converted and reshaped in the likeness of Christ

As born again, blood washed children of God, we are truly His treasure, encased in jars of clay! We glorify God when we acknowledge our dependence on Him, and turn to Him for our deliverance, and restoration.

As we remind ourselves that we are a treasure in jars of clay, call a family member / friend/acquaintance and share this scripture today. Also remind them that all power comes from God . . . "But we have this treasure in jars of clay to show that this all surpassing power is from God and not from us."

Give God praise for placing us in jars of clay, that are held in His hands.

## MY THOUGHTS AND MEDITATION

# *ROOM FOR YOU*

**Proverbs 18: 16**
A man's gift makes room for him, and brings him before great men.

There may be people we know, have seen or have heard of, who go to great lengths to get into organizations, or take unusual measures to meet famous or influential people. They manipulate, and will even pay for an introduction, to say they are friends with a prestigious person. Proverbs 18:16 tells us, whatever gift God has given you, He will place you in the presence of great men and women, in His perfect timing-if it is His will for you. We need to be conscious of the fact, that we are not always able to discern God's idea of "great". The person who has the greatest impact on our lives, may be one we would never have chosen, in the scheme of life! The expression, "What God has for me, is for me." is so true, because from the foundation of the world, God has already ordained what He has for you. Your gift will make room for you!

Romans 11: 29b, assures us—"For God's gifts and His call are irrevocable."

Each person has been given gifts according to God's choosing. In Matthew 25, there is the story of servants receiving various amounts to be taken care of, while their master was away. Each one did something different, according to how they felt they should have handled the masters money. Yet, I found it interesting that the bible said each one was given a talent, *"according to his own ability."*

What God has allotted to each of us, is **according to our ability**. May we focus on what we have, cultivate our gift(s), and God will reward us for how we handle, or do not handle, what He has already given to us.

Remember: Proverbs 18:16. "A man's/woman's gift makes room for him/her, and brings them before great men." How are you handling your gift?

**Colossians 3:1-2**
Since, then, you have been raised with Christ, set your hearts on things above, where Christ is seated at the right hand of God.
Set your minds on things above, not on earthly things. (NIV)

# MY THOUGHTS AND MEDITATION

# *SHUT THE DOOR*

**Matthew 25:10**
And while they went to buy, the bridegroom came, and those who were ready went in with him to the wedding, and the door was shut.

The parable of the "Ten Virgins" is about the second coming of Jesus Christ. Over three hundred times in scripture, we are told that Jesus Christ shall return, yet many are living as though this will never happen. In this parable, Jesus is depicted as "the bridegroom". Five of the virgins were prepared with oil, and five were unprepared to welcome Him. When the bridegroom arrived at midnight, those prepared with oil ushered Him to the wedding banquet, and the door was shut as they celebrated.

The five who were unprepared were shut out of the celebration. They had ample time to get ready, yet they did not see the urgency to prepare to be inside. Their decision cost them being shut out of the joy of the presence of the bride and bridegroom. Are you making decisions today that may cause the door to be shut, leaving you *outside* when the bridegroom comes? Do you need to "shut the door" on those things that will deny you entrance to the wedding banquet? Are you making plans for the great wedding spoken of in Revelations 21?

The Prophet David writes in Psalms 18:11, "You will show me the path of life; In Your presence is fullness of joy. At Your right hand are pleasures forevermore."

At the wedding banquet, we will rejoice forevermore, having eternal life with Him.

In Jesus name-SHUT THE DOOR!

## MY THOUGHTS AND MEDITATION

# *GOD STILL MOVES STONES*

**Mark 16:4**
"But when they looked up, they saw that the stone had been rolled away-for it was very large."

After the Sabbath was over and it was religiously appropriate to work and/or do any type of labor, the women, who were followers of Jesus, went to the tomb where he lay to anoint His body with spices. On the way, the women had a major, legitimate concern, "Who will roll away the very large stone that sealed the tomb?" Scripture eludes to the fact that their heads were bowed down as they walked along the road, for we read, "But when they **looked up**, they saw that the stone had been rolled away-for it was very large." These women knew that the stone was too large for them to roll away, but by faith, they journeyed on.

I rejoice each time I read this scripture, because it assures me over and over, that regardless of how large a "stone" in my path, I must journey on, and look up. By faith I am assured that God will send His angels to roll all stones away.

> Is there a "stone" in your path today?
> Rejoice that God still moves stones!

## *MY THOUGHTS AND MEDITATION*

# *BE AN ENCOURAGER*

**I Timothy 4:12**
Let no one despise your youth, but be an example to the believers in word, in conduct, in love, in spirit, in faith, in purity.

The Apostle Paul is giving this exhortation to his young spiritual son, Timothy. There are seven things Paul admonishes Timothy to do, and these seven points are still commendable for our youth today. First he says, be an example. Even though the news reporters sell on sensationalism, we still have young people who are excelling in many areas today. We need to launch a campaign, showcase and encourage our your youth and mentor them. This is what Paul did! Timothy is told to be an example to the **believers.** Why to believers? It is to encourage them along the way! Timothy is to be an **example** in **word, in conduct, in love, in spirit, in faith, in purity.**

That appears to be a HUGE order for a young person, but with God all things are possible. It is imperative that our words mirror our conduct; that we speak words that build up and not tear down. We are to be a reflection of Christ to the world, for we are to be "living epistles". This scripture is not only for youth, but adults as well.

Heavenly Host, show us the way to be an example in word, conduct, love, spirit, faith and in purity. You are our guide and leader and we release our will to your will. In Jesus name. Amen.

## MY THOUGHTS AND MEDITATION

# *ALL KNOWING GOD*

**Revelation 3:8**
"I know your works. See, I have set before you an open door, and no one can shut it, for you have a little strength, have kept My word, and have not denied My name."

I have heard that **everyone** has at least one skeleton in a closet that they cringe at the thought of the closet door being opened. There may also be a few closets that are being held closed by many, many hundreds of pounds of steel! Regardless of how the door is being held shut, God knows every act we have committed, by thought, word or deed. He says he knows our works, and he is faithful to forgive, through the blood of Jesus. If we keep His word and not deny His name, He will open doors that no man can shut, and close those doors that no man can open. Praise the Lord!

Holy Father, I thank and praise you for reminding us that you know our works. You are the One that even know our frame. We are also mindful that You created us in Your image. Thank you for allowing us to see that it was you that opened those doors that seemed impossible to transverse. We praise you that no one can shut us out of the divine destiny you have for our lives. Moreover, we exalt Your Holy name for closing doors that would lead to our destruction, if we entered in.

By Your Holy Spirit, empower us to continue to keep Your Word and never deny the precious name of Jesus.

In Jesus name we pray, Amen

## MY THOUGHTS AND MEDITATION

# *HIS BLESSING*

**Mark 10:16**
And He took the children in His arms, put His hands on them and blessed them."

The song says, "Jesus loves the little children", and in this scripture, Jesus takes children in His arms, loving holds them and blesses them. Psalms 127:3 tells us that, "Children are a heritage from the Lord"; but are we cherishing our children as a gift from the Lord, and are we taking the children in our arms and blessing them?

Children *are* a heritage from the Lord. They deserve and need a blessing. What a joy to see the wonder, innocence, and light in the eyes of a child discovering something "new" in this wonderful world. Social scientist and medical doctors have proven that babies thrive from being held and touched. It has also been shown that even adults need at least three hugs, or touches a day.

The expression, "Children are our future", should be changed to, "Children are our *present.*" Children are a **present** from God, and are our very **present** gift! Jesus shows us by example that children are valued and important in His sight. Can we do less?

Let us pray for children all over the world today, and bless them in Jesus' name.

## MY THOUGHTS AND MEDITATION

# *STEP OUT*

**Matthew 19: 28-29**
"And Peter answered Him and said, "Lord, if it is You, command me to come to you on the water." So He said, "Come." And when Peter had come down out of the boat, he walked on the water to go to Jesus.

Peter and the disciples were not sure that the vision walking on the water was Jesus, therefore he said, "Lord, *if* it is you, command me to come to you *on the water*." Peter had a personal relationship with Jesus, yet at that moment he was unsure of who Jesus was, and needed assurance of His identity. There are times when we too, struggle to see Jesus clearly because of life's many obstacles, yet He still bids us "Come". In obedience to the invitation of Jesus, Peter did something no one else has ever done, and that is, walk on water.

In meditating on this passage, I began to think of the many things we are able to do, when we are obedient to the command of Jesus. What is He calling me to do today that seems impossible? It was only when Peter took his eyes off Jesus that he began to sink. Have I begun to sink because I have taken my eyes off Jesus? Peter stepped out of the boat, by faith, and it is by faith that we too will do those things that seem impossible. Even though Peter momentarily took his eyes off Jesus and began to sink, Jesus never took His eyes off Peter.

In our own strength, and by our intellect, we will never achieve those things that may seem impossible, but by faith in the mighty power of God, all things are possible.

Do not concentrate on your weaknesses today, but step out and focus on the One that still bids us, "Come".

# MY THOUGHTS AND MEDITATION

# THE BLESSING

**Jude 1:1-2**
**To those who are called, sanctified by God the Father, and preserved in Jesus Christ. Mercy, peace and love be multiplied to you.**

Jude pronounces an awesome blessing upon a people. This blessing is specifically for "those who are called, sanctified by God the Father, and preserved in Jesus Christ." This blessing is for, "mercy, peace and love", to be multiplied to us; yes, given in abundance. Our world today is so filled with clamor, confusion, war, and threats of war, it is quite difficult to imagine mercy, peace and love being multiplied to us, yet the Psalmist clearly reminds us that, "He will keep you in perfect peace, whose mind is stayed on Thee."

Mercy has been applied to us by Christ' atoning death on the cross, so we are obligated to be merci- ful to others, instead of demanding justice when we feel we have been offended. Through His unconditional, unmerited love towards us, our gratitude should flow from the love that's been multiplied in our behalf. Just knowing we have been redeemed by the blood that Jesus shed for us, and resting in the assurance that every aspect of our lives are secure in His hands, we can have peace that passes all earthly understanding.

Today, may we reflect on the many ways that God the Father has multiplied His mercy, peace and love towards us, through Jesus Christ. Thank Him for calling us and sanctifying us, that we may receive this gracious blessing.

## MY THOUGHTS AND MEDITATION

## ALL SAINTS GOD'S HARVEST

**Luke 10: 2**
Then He said to them, "The harvest truly is great, but the laborers are few, therefore pray the lord of the harvest to send out laborers into His harvest."

Holy and Everlasting Father,
Empower us to sow good seed, in good soil, so that when You come to reap the harvest, there will be much fruit. In Jesus' name,
      Amen

**Philippians 4:6**
"Be anxious for nothing, but in everything by prayer and supplications, with thanksgiving, let you requests be made known to God."

# BLESSED FAITHFULNESS

**Hosea 6:3**
"Let us press on to know the Lord; his appearing is as sure as the dawn; He will come to us like the showers, like the spring rains that water the earth."

Hosea 6:1-3 is called "A call to repentance." The people had turned away from the Lord and were now being encouraged to return to him. There are times that we too, turn from the Lord. When you find yourself in that situation, let me encourage you to quickly return, to press on to really know the Lord. God is faithful to us every day, yet we often allow our agenda to get in the way of seeing how He blesses us, cares for us, and loves us unconditionally. Just meditate on this portion of scripture today: . . . His appearing is as sure as the dawn; He will come to us like the showers, like the spring rains that water the earth."

Father God, quicken us in spirit that we may have a sincere heart to press on to know you in spirit and in truth. The earth responds to your loving care as you send down the rain by producing foliage, and food for us. We pray that we too will respond in thanksgiving and praise for your faithfulness every day. Thank you Lord and we praise your Holy name. Amen

# *MY THOUGHTS AND MEDITATION*

# *PRAISE AND THANKSGIVING*

**Psalms 107:15**
"Oh, that men would give thanks to the Lord for His goodness, and for His wonderful works to the children of men!"

The 107th Psalms is known as "The Psalms of the Redeemed." What a joy! We can do something that the angels in heaven cannot do; we can give thanks and praise God for redeeming us. We can give thanks for His wonderful works to the children of men. The Psalmist himself said, "I will bless the Lord at all times; His praise shall continuously be in my mouth (Psalms 34:1). He further encourages us in Psalms 147:1 with these words, "Praise the Lord! For it is pleasant, and praise is beautiful."

The Apostle Paul tells us, that there are times our thanks and praise may even be a sacrifice (Hebrews 13:15) "Therefore by Him, let us continually offer the sacrifice of praise to God, that is, the fruit of our lips, giving thanks to His name". He then adds, in verse 16, "But do not forget to do good and to share, for with such sacrifices God is well pleased." My fellow Sojourners, have you paused today to thank and praise God for His goodness and His wonderful works? Offer up a sweet smelling sacrifice of thanksgiving and praise-even the fruit of our lips. Be doers of the Word, and not hearers only (James 1:22).

Blessed Redeemer of our soul, We pray that all will give you thanks. We bless the wonderful name of Jesus, who freed us from sin and condemnation, by your precious blood. In the name of Jesus. Amen.

## MY THOUGHTS AND MEDITATION

# *EXAMINE YOUR FRUIT*

**Luke 6:43,44**
For a good tree does not bear bad fruit; nor does a bad tree bear good fruit. For every tree is known by it's own fruit.

As a young girl growing up, I heard many "proverbs" quoted in my home. My mother had a way of speaking to us in "proverbs". One of the expressions I heard often was, "An apple doesn't fall far from the tree." This was usually quoted when someone from a family with unsavory history would commit an infraction that was a reflection of this family. This expression was also used if a person excelled in a particular area.

Today we read the words of Jesus in Luke 6:43,44. "A good tree does not bear bad fruit; nor does a bad tree bear good fruit. For every tree is known by its own fruit." Let us take a few moments to examine our "fruit". Are there blemishes on the fruit, rotten places, worm holes, bruises or soft spots? Or is the fruit edible?

Every tree needs to be pruned, and the soil fertilized at some time. Trees also need spraying for insects/bugs/mites that may kill it. We too can be "infected" by negative influences in our lives. Every spiritual tree needs to be cared for by the Master Husbandman; the One who said, "I am the vine, you are the branches; without Me you can do nothing."

It's time to examine our tree and examine the fruit we are bearing. Amen.

# MY THOUGHTS AND MEDITATION

# *IT'S WITHIN YOU*

**Luke 17:21**
Once, having been asked by the Pharisee when the kingdom of God would come, Jesus replied, "The kingdom of God does not come with your careful observations, nor will people say 'Here it is', or 'There it is', because **the kingdom of God is within you."**

The number of "self help" books on the market has risen to astronomical figures. People are seeking ways to improve themselves and/or find help for the void they feel in their lives. We tend to look outside ourselves, instead of seeking the God within us. The bible tells us we are made in the image of God, and Jesus Himself said that His spirit (the Holy Spirit) lives within us.

Through reading God's Word, meditating on His Word, and through prayer, the kingdom of God will manifest itself through each of us. We pray, "Thy kingdom come, Thy will be done, on earth . . . ."; We are the vessels that God will use to usher in His kingdom. Our task is to begin living as kingdom people, on earth.

How are we reflecting the kingdom of God within?

## *MY THOUGHTS AND MEDITATION*

# *THERE IS A CHAMPION IN YOU*

**Romans 8:37**
Yet in all these things, we are more than conquerors through Him (Christ Jesus) who loves us.

Today, by the power of the Holy Spirit, I declare, "There is a champion in you!" What is a champion? A champion is not only a winner, but someone who has won in a spectacular way. A champion may also be someone who has persevered in spite of all odds. Each day an African American male survives the drug culture, does not drop out of school, be- come an abuser, an unwed father, or engage in risky behavior, he is a champion. When our young ladies are not engaged in similar behavior-they are champions too; for we all want to be a champion.

Being a mentor to a young person, will also qualify you as a champion. As adults, we can share our life experiences and help young people avoid pitfalls. Consider sharing this scripture, for it may impact a young life: "For I know the plans I have for you," declares the Lord, "plans to prosper you and not to harm you, plans to give you hope and a future. Then you will call upon me and come and pray to me, and I will listen to you. You will seek me and find me when you seek me with all your heart. I will be found by you," declares the Lord, "and will bring you back from captivity . . ." Jeremiah 29: 9-14a Declare to young people in your midst-THERE IS A CHAMPION IN YOU.

Father God, Help us to be the champion you said we are through Christ Jesus. May we conquer all evil forces that may thwart the plans you have for us. Thank you for your promises. Amen.

# *MY THOUGHTS AND MEDITATION*

# *INTERCESSORS*

**Acts 12:5**
Peter therefore was kept in prison: but prayer was made without ceasing of the church unto God for him. (Read all of Acts 12)

Intercessory prayer was made by the church members in Peter's behalf. We read further that God sent an angel to release Peter from the jail, where he was chained and in stocks. This deliverance from jail was nothing less than a miracle.

When was the last time your church came together for no other reason than to unite in intercessory prayer? When was the last time you fervently prayed for someone?

Because of intercessory prayer, Peter was released from jail. We too must be clear that God still uses intercessors. Our prayers may possibly be the call that God needs to move in behalf of a soul in distress. There are many types of chains that have folk bound. They may be chained to substance abuse, domestic abuse, child abuse, sexual abuse; chained to past experiences, mental anguish, etc. etc. God bends His ear-listening for our prayer.

Our Father, who art in heaven; hallowed be Thy name, Thy kingdom come Thy will be done, on earth as it is in heaven. Give us this day, our daily bread. And forgive us our trespasses as we forgive those who trespass against us. And lead us not into temptation, but deliver us from evil. For Thine is the kingdom, the power and the glory, forever. Amen.

## MY THOUGHTS AND MEDITATION

# THIS TIME HE CAME DOWN

**Luke 6: 17-18**
"And He came down with them and stood on a level place with a crowd of His disciples and a great multitude of people from all Judea and Jerusalem, and from the sea-coast of Tyre and Sidon, who came to hear Him and be healed of their diseases, as well as those troubled by evil spirits were cured, and the people all tried to touch him, because power was coming from Him and healing them all."

Prior to these verses, the bible tells us that Jesus had been on a mountain all night in prayer. It was the morning after this all-night prayer vigil that Jesus chose His twelve disciples. He then continued walking down the mountain until He reached **level ground.** People came from all around, even from the sea-coast to be healed, to touch Jesus for the healing power He possessed. The scripture says, "He healed every one", even those suffering from emotional, and psychological illness.

Notice, Jesus came down on **level ground** to meet the needs of the people, and Jesus still comes to level ground to meet our needs. Have faith to reach out and touch Him, for you too may be healed! Rejoice that Jesus is presently within our reach; and He still heals. "Jesus Christ, the same, yesterday, today and forever."

He touched me, Oh He touched me. And, Oh the joy that floods my soul. Something happened and now I know, He touched me and made me whole." As we kneel on level ground, pray for His healing touch for all in need.

## *MY THOUGHTS AND MEDITATION*

# THE CALL

**Isaiah 43:1**
"But now, thus says the Lord, who created you, O Jacob, and He who formed you, O Israel: "Fear not, for I have redeemed you. **I have called you by your name**; you are mine."

I am sure each of us have been called at some time in our lives and we were unprepared to answer, or did not want to answer. I remember as a child, when my mother called us by our full name, we had best come running. That was a call! God called many people for various tasks. Some were called by name, and others simply submitted to the voice of God when they heard His directives within their heart. Abraham was called to go to a land he knew not. Miriam was called to lead the women to dance in victory. Noah was called to build an ark even though it had never rained. God called Samuel when he was a young lad. John the Baptist was called to tell the people to repent and be baptized. Mary was called to bear the Son of God (what a call), then God called Jesus to be our Redeemer and Savior. Each call was part of God's great plan.

God is calling you to carry out His plan for your life. By answering His call, you will be blessed and a blessing to others.

Omnipotent Savior,
    Today we pray that we will hear, recognize and answer Your call. In Jesus' name. Amen.

## MY THOUGHTS AND MEDITATION

# *HUMBLE YOUR SOUL*

**Joel 2:12-13**
Now, therefore, says the Lord, "Return to me with all your heart, with fasting, with weeping, and with mourning; rend your hearts, and not your clothing. Return to the Lord you God. For He is gracious and merciful, slow to anger, and of great kindness; and He relents from doing harm."

As we move further into our Twenty-One Day Spiritual Journey, God says consider fasting". There are a multitude of spiritual benefits from refraining from food; among those benefits are divine direction, repentance and strength for our Christian journey. The Prophet Joel tells the people what God wants them to do, and reminds them of God's attributes. The Psalmist said, "I humbled **my soul** with fasting"(Psalms 5:13) Food and water are necessary for sustaining life, but when we purpose in our hearts to refrain from food for a specific time period, we are saying in essence, "Lord, sustain me, feed me with Living Bread, I want more of You than anything else."

Jesus said in Matthew 6:17, "But *when you fast*, anoint your head and wash your face, so that you do not appear to men to be fasting, but to your Father who is in the secret place; and your Father who sees in secret **will reward you openly.**" This scripture assures us that Jesus expects us to fast, and do it without fanfare and/or telling others.

For a "breakthrough" in your spiritual life, fasting and prayer, is the way. Today, consider fasting as part of your spiritual discipline. (Books on fasting are available at Christian Book Stores)

## MY THOUGHTS AND MEDITATION

**1 Peter 2:9**
"But you are a chosen generation, a royal priesthood, a holy nation, His own special people, that you may proclaim the praises of Him who called you out of darkness into His marvelous light."

Get Published, Inc!
Thorofare, NJ 08086
02 March, 2010
BA2010061

## THE ANSWER IS FOUND IN DOING THREE THINGS

What must I do
    to insure peace of mind?
Is the answer I'm seeking
    too hard to find?
How can I know
    what GOD wants me to be?
How can I tell
    what's expected of me?
Where can I go
    for guidance and aid
To help me correct
    the errors I've made
The answer is found
    in doing three things
And great is the gladness
    that doing them brings—
Do justice—love kindness—
    walk humbly with GOD.
For with these three things
    as your "rule and your rod"
All things worth having
    are yours to achieve
If you follow GOD'S words
    and have FAITH to BELIEVE.

        Helen Steiner Rice
        Poems of Faith

# SERMON

*Scripture(s)*_____

*Subject*_____

*Notes*_____

_____
_____
_____
_____
_____
_____
_____
_____
_____
_____
_____
_____
_____
_____
_____
_____
_____
_____
_____

**Point of the message**

_____
_____
_____